I WAS THE PROBLEM BECAUSE YOU NEEDED ONE

BEING THE BLACK SHEEP AND BREAKING THE CYCLE

CHARLES B.F. BROOKS

EPIGRAPH

Charles B. F. Brooks

"A raw, blunt memoir about being blamed for everything, loved conditionally, and finally choosing help before the pain became a weapon."

I was the scapegoat my family needed—until the rage nearly made me become exactly what they said I was.

PREFACE: WHY I'M SAYING THIS OUT LOUD

I'm not writing this to sound tough. I'm writing it because it's true.

For most of my life, I carried stories I wasn't supposed to tell. Not because they were secrets, exactly, but because speaking them out loud felt like betrayal. In my family, in my community, you kept your pain private. You didn't air dirty laundry. You didn't talk about what happened behind closed doors. And you definitely didn't go to therapy—that was for white people, for "crazy" people, for people who couldn't handle their problems on their own. So I handled it. I swallowed the anger, packed down the hurt, smiled when I was supposed to smile, and stayed quiet when I was supposed to stay quiet. I became good at pretending everything was fine, even when my insides were screaming. I learned to be the problem they needed me to be, and then I learned to hate myself for it.

This book exists because silence almost killed me. Not literally—though there were moments that came close. But silence has a way of rotting you from the inside out. It turns pain into poison. It makes you believe that the way you were treated was normal, deserved, or somehow your fault. And when you're a Black kid growing up in a community where everyone's supposed to be strong, where asking for help is seen as weakness, where parents are treated like gods who can never be questioned—that silence can become a life sentence.

I was the black sheep. The problem child. The one who never measured up, no matter how hard I tried. I was blamed for things I didn't do, compared to kids whose parents actually showed up for them, and expected to succeed without any of the support those same kids took for granted. I grew up feeling unwanted, unworthy, and unwelcome in my own family. And nobody—not one adult—ever asked me how I was really doing. Instead, they told me what I was going to become. A thief. A failure. Nothing. And when you hear that enough times from the people who are supposed to love you, you start to believe it. You start to act it out. You start becoming the prophecy they spoke over your life, because at least then you're in control of something.

But here's the thing about prophecies: they only come true if nobody interrupts them. This memoir is my interruption.

It's the story of abandonment and survival, of watching other kids get the love I was denied, of living through years of mental and physical abuse that nobody outside that house would believe. It's about the rage that built up inside me, the dangerous thoughts I had, and the moment I realized that if I didn't get help, I was going to become exactly what they always said I was—or worse.

This book is for every Black kid who grew up being the scapegoat. For every parent who thinks being stern means being silent, who thinks discipline means dominance, who thinks asking for help is a sign of weakness instead of wisdom. It's for the people who were told to pray the pain away, to be strong, to get over it—and who are still carrying wounds that never healed because nobody taught them they were allowed to ask for help.

I'm not writing this as someone who has it all figured out. I'm writing this as someone who barely survived not figuring it out. I'm writing this because I know what it feels like to sit in the dark and fantasize about violence, to feel so consumed by rage that you scare yourself, to realize that untreated pain doesn't just go away—it metastasizes. And I'm writing this because I refuse to let the cycle continue.

Breaking generational trauma doesn't require perfection. It doesn't require a happy ending tied up with a bow. It requires honesty. It requires someone being willing to say: this hurt me, and I'm choosing to do something about it before I pass it on.

So that's what this is. An honest account of what happens when children are treated like problems instead of people, when love is conditional, when help is stigmatized, and when rage is left to ferment in the dark. It's also about what happens when you finally, finally ask for help—not because you're weak, but because you're tired of being broken.

If you've ever been the one everyone blamed, the one expected to be strong while no one protected you, the one who learned to survive instead of live—this book is for you. If you're a parent who was raised with the "we don't do therapy" mentality and you're wondering if there's another way—this book is for you, too.

This is my truth. I'm saying it out loud because silence is what almost killed me. And because someone, somewhere, needs permission to stop being silent, too.

PART I

THE MAKING

1

I BARELY KNOW HER

A child who doesn't feel wanted will find ways to not care first.

I was five, maybe six years old, when another kid tried to hurt me by insulting my mother. We were outside, in that stretch of cracked pavement between Grandmother's house and the neighbors', where all the kids in the neighborhood gathered to play. I don't remember what we were arguing about—probably something stupid, the kind of thing kids fight over and forget an hour later. But I remember the moment he thought he'd won. He puffed up his chest, pointed at me, and said something nasty about Mother. I don't even remember the exact words. What I remember is the look on his face, that smug certainty that he'd just delivered the killing blow. He expected me to crumble. To cry, maybe. To run inside and tell on him.

Instead, I looked him dead in the eye and said: "I don't care. I barely know her."

The other kids got quiet. I don't think they expected that. I don't think I expected that. But it was true, and the truth came out plain and simple, the way it does when you're too young to know you're supposed to lie about things like that. I barely knew her. Mother wasn't a presence in my life. She was a name, a face I saw sometimes, a person I was told was supposed to matter but who mostly felt like a character in someone else's story. Grandmother raised me. Grandmother was the one who fed me, who put me to bed, who yelled at me when I messed up. Mother was somewhere else, doing something else, living a life that didn't include much space for me. So when that kid tried to use her as a weapon against me, it didn't land. You can't hurt someone with something they don't have.

The boy didn't know what to say after that. He just stood there, deflated, and eventually we all went back to playing. But I remember the weight of those words in my mouth: I barely know her. I remember how easy they were to say. I remember not feeling sad about it.

That should've been a red flag. A child shouldn't be able to say something like that without flinching. But nobody asked me about it. Nobody pulled me aside and said, "Hey, are you okay? Do you feel loved? Do you know that you matter?" Nobody thought to check. And so I learned early that my normal wasn't something people questioned. It was just the way things were.

When you grow up without your parents, people like to tell you that you're lucky to have your grandmother. And don't get me wrong —Grandmother kept me alive. She kept a roof over my head and food in my stomach. But surviving isn't the same as thriving. And a grandmother doing her daughter's job isn't the same as a mother choosing to show up.

Mother didn't choose me. I felt that every single day. She didn't call to check on me. She didn't send birthday cards or Christmas presents. She didn't show up to school events or ask how I was doing. And when she did come around, it felt performative, like she was checking a box or fulfilling an obligation someone else had put on her. I used to watch other kids with their moms and wonder what I was doing wrong. Why didn't mine want me? What was it about me that made it so easy for her to stay away?

Children aren't supposed to ask themselves those questions. But I did. And when you don't have answers, you start making them up.

You start believing that maybe you're the problem. Maybe you're too much, or not enough, or wrong in some fundamental way that makes you unlovable. That belief doesn't just go away when you grow up. It calcifies. It becomes part of how you see yourself, part of how you move through the world. You become the kid who doesn't expect anyone to show up, because nobody ever has.

Years later, after I was grown, Mother would complain that I never called her. That I didn't check on her, didn't come around enough, didn't act like a good son. The hypocrisy was staggering. She never called me as a child. Never checked on me. Never came around unless someone made her. But somehow, I was supposed to chase after her, to beg for the relationship she never built, to give her the love and attention she never gave me. It didn't work like that. You can't abandon someone and then demand their loyalty. You can't ghost a child and then guilt-trip the adult they become.

That moment on the pavement when I said "I barely know her" was the first time I realized I could protect myself by not caring. If I didn't care, I couldn't be hurt. If I didn't expect anything, I couldn't be disappointed. It was a survival mechanism. But survival mechanisms have a cost. When you teach yourself not to care, you don't get to turn it off when you want to. It seeps into everything. You stop expecting love. You stop believing you're worth it. You start treating relationships like transactions, always waiting for the other shoe to drop, always looking for the exit.

That's what abandonment does. It doesn't just leave a hole where love should be. It teaches you that the hole is normal, that wanting more is foolish, that you should be grateful for scraps. And when you're a kid, you don't have the language to say: This isn't normal. This is hurting me. I need help. You just live with it. You adapt. You become smaller, quieter, harder.

But surviving isn't living. And it sure as hell isn't healing.

I want to say something about Grandmother here, because the story doesn't end with the woman who kept me alive. Years later, when I was deep in therapy, my counselor asked about my relationship with her. I'd always glossed over it—she fed me, she housed me, she kept the lights on. What else was there to say? But the therapist pressed: "Did she see you? Not as a responsibility. As a person."

I sat with that for a long time. The honest answer was: I don't know. I don't know if Grandmother was capable of that kind of seeing, or if she was so worn down by life and by her own daughter's failures that she had nothing left to give. I never got to ask her. She was gone before I did that work. What I know is that she was complicated—not a villain, not a savior. A tired woman doing an impossible job, sometimes with cruelty, sometimes with something that looked like care. I've had to make peace with not knowing whether she loved me. That ambiguity is its own kind of grief.

Takeaway: **When a child stops caring, it's not strength—it's a wound that nobody noticed.**

2

THE BLACK SHEEP CURRICULUM

Some kids are raised. Others are trained to fail.

I don't know exactly when I became the black sheep. Maybe I was born into the role. Maybe it was assigned the moment Mother handed me off to Grandmother and walked away. All I know is that by the time I was old enough to understand the word "disappointment," I already knew I was one. Everything I did was wrong. Everything I didn't do was wrong. I was too loud, too quiet, too slow, too fast, too much, not enough. I was compared to other kids constantly—kids whose parents actually parented them, who had support and structure and someone checking their homework. Kids who got told "I love you" and "I'm proud of you" and "You can do this." I got told what I wasn't.

"Why can't you be more like Cousin? Why can't you sit still like Neighbor's Kid? Why can't you do better? What's wrong with you?"

Nobody ever answered that last question. They just kept asking it, over and over, until I started asking it myself. What is wrong with me?

The thing about being the black sheep is that it becomes a self-fulfilling prophecy. When you're constantly told you're the problem, you start acting like it. When nobody expects anything good from you, you stop trying to prove them wrong. Why bother? You're damned if you do, damned if you don't. So you lean into it. You become the class clown, the troublemaker, the kid who doesn't care. You make people laugh because at least that way they're paying attention to you for something other than what you did wrong. You act out because at least when you're in trouble, you're visible. Negative attention is still attention. And when you're starving for it, you take what you can get.

But here's what nobody tells you: that survival strategy will follow you for the rest of your life. The class clown becomes the adult who can't be serious. The troublemaker becomes the adult who self-sabotages. The kid who stops trying becomes the adult who doesn't believe they deserve success. You carry the curriculum they taught you. And if nobody interrupts it, you'll teach it to your own kids.

I remember sitting at Grandmother's kitchen table, maybe nine or ten years old, staring at homework I didn't understand. I'd been sitting there for an hour, stuck on the same problem, too afraid to ask for help because asking for help meant admitting I was stupid. Grandmother walked past, glanced at the paper, and sighed. Not the kind of sigh that says let me help you. The kind that says of course you don't get it.

"You need to focus," she said. "Stop playing around and pay attention."

I wasn't playing around. I was stuck. But explaining that felt pointless. She'd already decided I wasn't trying hard enough. I thought about the kids at school whose parents sat with them, walked them through problems, hired tutors when they struggled. I thought about Cousin, whose dad checked his homework every night, who took him to the library on weekends, who made learning feel like something worth doing. Nobody checked my homework. Nobody took me to the library. Nobody made me feel like I was capable of learning, or that struggling was normal, or that needing help didn't mean I was broken. They just expected me to figure it out. And when I couldn't, they acted like it was proof of what they already believed: that I wasn't good enough.

The comparisons were relentless. Cousin got good grades. Why couldn't I? Neighbor's Kid stayed out of trouble. Why couldn't I? Friend was respectful, responsible, mature. Why wasn't I? What they didn't say—what they never acknowledged—was that those kids had parents who showed up. Parents who helped with homework, who talked to teachers, who set boundaries with love instead of anger. I didn't have that. But I was still expected to produce the same results. It was like being handed a broken tool and then being punished for not building a house. The game was rigged from the start, but nobody cared.

Here's the thing about being constantly compared: it kills your confidence. You stop believing you're capable of anything good. You start to believe that the problem isn't the lack of support or guidance or love—it's you. You're defective. You're the common denominator. And once you believe that, it's almost impossible to unlearn. I carried that belief into everything. School. Friendships. Relationships. Jobs. Every time something went wrong, my first thought was: Of course. It's me. I'm the problem. Even when I wasn't.

The worst part wasn't the comparisons themselves. It was the hypocrisy. They wanted me to succeed, but they didn't give me the tools. They wanted me to be respectful, but they didn't model respect. They wanted me to believe in myself, but they never believed in me first. They wanted the outcome without putting in the work. And when I failed to deliver, they acted like I was the one who'd let them down. That's not parenting. That's setting someone up to fail and then blaming them for it.

Years later, I'd realize that being the black sheep wasn't about me. It was about them. They needed someone to blame, someone to project their frustrations onto, someone to make them feel better about their own choices. I was convenient. I was young, powerless, and already positioned outside the circle of approval. So I became the dumping ground for everything they didn't want to face about themselves. But when you're a kid, you don't know that. You just know that you're not enough. And that knowledge becomes a weight you carry everywhere.

Takeaway: **You can't expect a child to thrive in soil you never watered.**

3

PROPHECIES HURT MORE THAN PUNCHES

Words don't fade like bruises do.

Grandmother said it once, and I never forgot it. "You're never going to be anything more than a thief." I don't remember what I'd done to prompt it. Probably something small, something a normal kid does—taking a cookie without asking, or pocketing change I found on the counter. The kind of thing you correct with a conversation, not a curse. But Grandmother didn't correct. She prophesied. And when the person raising you tells you who you're going to become, you believe them. Because if they can't see anything good in you, maybe there isn't anything good to see.

I was maybe nine years old when she said it. Old enough to understand the words, young enough to think adults always told the truth. Old enough to feel the weight of it settle into my chest like a stone. A thief. That's all you'll ever be. Not: "That was wrong, and here's why." Not: "I'm disappointed, but I know you can do better." Not even: "We need to talk about this." Just: You're a thief. That's your destiny. I see your future, and it's empty.

There's a special kind of pain that comes from being condemned by the people who are supposed to protect you. Physical pain fades. Bruises heal. But words like that? They burrow in. They take root.

They grow into beliefs you carry for decades, shaping how you see yourself and what you think you deserve. I didn't just hear Grandmother say I was a thief. I heard her say I was worthless. I heard her say she'd given up on me. I heard her say that no matter what I did, I'd never be more than the worst thing she imagined I could be. And I was nine years old.

After that, I started believing it. Not consciously—I didn't wake up and think, Guess I'll be a thief today. But subconsciously, it shaped me. It became a lens I looked through. When I messed up, it was proof. When I got in trouble, it was inevitable. When I made bad choices, it was because that's what thieves do. I stopped fighting the narrative. If that's who they thought I was, fine. If that's all they expected from me, why try to be anything else? That's what prophecies do. They don't just predict the future. They create it.

The thing is, kids need adults to believe in them. Not blindly, not without accountability, but with the foundational assumption that they're capable of good. That they have potential. That mistakes are part of learning, not proof of permanent failure. When you take that away—when you tell a child they're destined for nothing—you don't just hurt them. You cripple them. You steal their ability to imagine a better version of themselves.

Grandmother didn't mean to destroy me. I don't think she woke up that day planning to wound me in a way that would last twenty years. But she did. Because she didn't realize that her words had power. She didn't realize that I would remember them long after she forgot she said them.

I've thought a lot about why she said it. Was she just tired? Was she dealing with her own pain and lashing out at the easiest target? Was she repeating something someone once said to her? I don't know. And honestly, it doesn't matter. Understanding why someone hurt you doesn't undo the hurt. What matters is that it happened. What matters is that no one stepped in to contradict her, to tell me she was wrong, to say: "You're not a thief. You're a kid who made a mistake, and mistakes don't define you." What matters is that I was left to carry that label alone.

Years later, when I started getting into real trouble, I wasn't surprised. I'd been told this was coming. I'd been prepared for failure my whole life. So when it arrived, it almost felt like relief. Like, See? They were right. This is who I am. That's the cruelest part of a prophecy: even when you hate it, part of you wants to fulfill it. Because at least then you're in control. At least then you're meeting expectations, even if the expectations are garbage.

It took me a long time to realize that I didn't have to be what they said I was. That their words were never about me—they were about their own limitations, their own fears, their own failures. They couldn't see past their pain, so they projected it onto me. But by the time I figured that out, I'd already spent years living like the prophecy was law.

Here's what I wish someone had told me: Your family's words are not the truth. They're just their version of it, filtered through their own wounds and biases and limitations. You are not what they call you. You are not the worst thing they imagine you could be. You are not the sum of their disappointments. You are a person. A whole, complex, evolving person. And the fact that they can't see that says more about them than it does about you.

Takeaway: **The words you speak over a child become the voice in their head—choose them carefully.**

4

WATCHING OTHER KIDS GET LOVED

Hunger doesn't always look like hunger.

I grew up in a small community where a lot of kids were being raised by their grandmothers. So I wasn't alone in that. But I was alone in something else: the absence of my parents wasn't just physical. It was absolute. Other kids had parents who were gone but not gone. Fathers who didn't live with them but who called, who sent money, who showed up on birthdays. Mothers who were working in another city but who came home on weekends, who made sure their kid knew they were loved. My parents were ghosts. Present enough to exist, absent enough that I had to explain their existence. And I noticed. I noticed everything.

I noticed when Cousin got new shoes. Name-brand ones, the kind kids showed off at school. I asked him where they came from. "My dad," he said, casual, like it was the most normal thing in the world. I looked down at my shoes—secondhand, scuffed, too big because Grandmother bought them a size up so I could grow into them.

I noticed when Friend came back from a weekend trip. He'd gone to an amusement park with his dad. He talked about the rides, the junk food, the way his dad won him a stuffed animal at one of the games. "What'd you do this weekend?" he asked me. "Nothing," I said.

I noticed when Neighbor's Kid got in trouble at school and his mom showed up to the parent-teacher conference. She was upset with him, sure, but she was there. She talked to the teacher, made a plan, grounded him, but also told him she loved him and knew he could do better. When I got in trouble, Grandmother yelled at me and told me I was going to end up in jail. Nobody showed up to the conference. Nobody made a plan. Nobody said, "I love you, but this has to stop." I noticed. And every time I noticed, it hurt.

The worst part wasn't the absence itself. It was the reminder that I wasn't worth showing up for. Other kids' parents checked on them. Called them. Sent cards. Bought them gifts. Made them feel like they mattered. Mine didn't. And when you're a kid, you don't rationalize that away. You think, What's wrong with me? Why didn't Father call? Was I not important enough? Why didn't Mother send birthday presents? Did she forget I existed?

I watched other kids get loved, and I felt like I was watching through glass. Close enough to see it, too far away to touch it.

There was this one time—I must've been about seven—when Cousin got a package in the mail. His dad had sent it: a new video game, some candy, a card that said "Love you, kiddo." Cousin opened it at Grandmother's house, and I sat there watching, trying to keep my face neutral. Trying not to let anyone see how much it hurt. "Your dad's cool," I said, because that's what you're supposed to say. "Yeah," Cousin said, already focused on the game.

I went outside after that. Sat on the steps and stared at the street, waiting for a car that wasn't coming. Waiting for someone to pull up and say, "Surprise, I was thinking about you." Nobody came. I don't think anyone noticed I left. And even if they did, they wouldn't have understood why. Because from the outside, I looked fine. I had food, shelter, a grandmother who kept me alive. But being kept alive isn't the same as being loved.

I used to fantasize about it. About Father showing up with gifts, taking me somewhere, just the two of us. About Mother calling and asking how I was doing, really listening, really caring. But fantasies don't fix anything. They just make the real world hurt more. Because in the real world, Father didn't show up. Mother didn't call. And the longer it went on, the more I stopped expecting them to. Eventually, I stopped fantasizing. I stopped waiting. I stopped hoping. And that's when the anger started.

Here's what I didn't understand then: I wasn't angry because I was bad. I was angry because I was hurt. And hurt that big, in a body that small, with no one to help me process it? It doesn't just sit quietly. It looks for an exit. It explodes. But I didn't know that. I just knew I was angry all the time, and I didn't know why, and nobody asked. They just told me to calm down. To behave. To be grateful for what I had. But gratitude doesn't fill the hole where love should be.

Takeaway: **A child who watches other kids get love they're denied doesn't forget—they just learn not to expect it.**

5

THE DOOR WAS AJAR

Sometimes closeness is just a crack of light away.

Father came to visit once. I don't remember why. Maybe Grandmother called him, maybe it was guilt, maybe it was obligation. I just remember the evening he showed up—late, maybe nine or nine-thirty—and the way my heart jumped when I saw him on the couch. I was supposed to be in bed. But I couldn't sleep. Not when he was out there. So I cracked the door. Just enough to see into the living room. Just enough to watch him.

He was sitting on the couch, staring at the TV, bathed in that blue flickering light. He looked tired. Distant. But he was there, and that was more than usual. I sat on the floor just inside my room, my back against the doorframe, and I watched him. I wasn't trying to be sneaky. I just wanted to be near him.

I don't know how long I sat there. Long enough that I started to imagine what I'd say if he noticed me. Maybe he'd call me over. Maybe we'd sit together, and he'd ask me about school or tell me a story or just let me exist next to him. I wasn't asking for much. I just wanted him to see me.

But then he did see me. And it didn't go the way I'd imagined. He turned his head, looked right at me, and his face hardened.

"What are you doing up?"

His voice wasn't warm. It wasn't curious. It was annoyed. I froze.

"I—"

"You're supposed to be in bed. Go."

That was it. No "come here." No "can't sleep?" No acknowledgment that maybe, just maybe, I wanted to spend time with him. Just: Go.

I don't remember walking back to bed. I just remember the feeling. Disappointment doesn't cover it. Disappointment is when you expect something and it doesn't happen. This was worse. This was being seen and still being dismissed. This was realizing that even when he knew I wanted him, he didn't want me back.

I think about that night a lot. I think about how simple it would've been for him to do something different. To say, "Come here, sit with me for a minute." To ask, "What's on your mind?" He didn't have to have all the answers. He didn't have to be perfect. He just had to try. But he didn't. He sent me away. And in doing so, he taught me that wanting him was something to be ashamed of.

I've spent years trying to understand what was happening inside him that night. Maybe he was ashamed—of his absence, of not knowing what to say to a kid he'd barely raised. Maybe closeness scared him the same way it eventually scared me: he'd learned somewhere that needing people was weakness, and seeing me reach for him from that doorway felt like a mirror he didn't want to look into. I don't know. He never said. But I think about it because it matters—because a man who can send his child back to bed without a word isn't indifferent so much as he's terrified. And terrified people hurt the people who need them most.

That moment crystallized something I'd been feeling for years but hadn't been able to name: I wasn't just unwanted. I was inconvenient. My need for connection, for attention, for love—it was a burden. So I stopped asking for it. I stopped sitting by doors. I stopped waiting for visits. I stopped hoping. Because hope, I'd learned, was just another word for disappointment waiting to happen.

Here's the thing about kids: they don't need grand gestures. They don't need expensive gifts or elaborate plans. They just need presence. They need to feel like their existence matters to you, like spending time with them isn't a chore. Father could've given me five minutes. Five minutes to show me that I was worth his time. But he didn't. And I never forgot it.

That night taught me that wanting closeness was dangerous. That vulnerability would be punished. That it was safer to be distant, detached, armored. And I carried that lesson into every relationship I ever had. I became the person who left first, who didn't ask for anything, who never admitted I needed anyone. Because the last time I admitted I needed someone, they sent me back to bed.

Takeaway: **A child sitting at a cracked door isn't misbehaving—they're asking to be wanted.**

PART II

THE BREAKING

6

WHEN LOVE TURNED INTO A BILL

The cruelest manipulation is making someone pay for affection they were owed for free.

Mother started caring about me the moment I got a job. Not when I was five and learning to read. Not when I was ten and struggling in school. Not when I was fifteen and getting into trouble. But when I turned eighteen, graduated high school, and started bringing home a paycheck—that's when I suddenly mattered.

She reached out. She wanted me to come live with her. At first, I thought it meant something. I thought maybe she'd changed. Maybe she regretted the years of absence. I was wrong.

The first month felt almost normal. She cooked dinner sometimes. We watched TV together. She asked about my job, about my day. It felt like what I'd always wanted: a mother who cared. But then the requests started. "Can you help with rent this month?" I said yes. "I need some money for groceries." Okay. "The electric bill is higher than I thought. Can you cover the difference?" I kept saying yes. Because I wanted her to keep wanting me around. Because I was finally getting her attention, and I didn't want to lose it.

But the requests didn't stop. They escalated. Every week, there was something new. A bill she couldn't cover. An expense she didn't plan for. Money she needed right now, today, or something bad would happen. And if I hesitated—if I said I didn't have it—her whole demeanor changed. The warmth disappeared. She got cold, sharp, distant. She didn't yell. She didn't have to. She just withdrew. And that withdrawal was a weapon. It said: If you don't give me what I want, I'll stop pretending to love you.

I started giving her more than I should. More than I could afford. I was young, working a low-paying job, trying to save, trying to build something. But she always needed more. And the worst part? She framed it like I owed her. "After everything I've done for you," she'd say. As if she'd been there. As if she'd raised me. She hadn't done anything for me. Grandmother had raised me. Mother had been a ghost. But now that I had money, suddenly she was my mother, and I was the ungrateful son who didn't appreciate her.

The manipulation was elegant. She never said, "Give me your money." She said, "I'm struggling." She said, "I don't know what I'm going to do." She said it in a way that made me feel guilty for having anything she didn't. And when guilt didn't work, she used fear. "I might get evicted if I can't pay rent." "The lights are going to get shut off." She made her survival my responsibility. And because I was young and desperate for her approval, I took it on.

One night, I told her I couldn't give her money that week. I'd just paid my own bills, and I was broke. She looked at me with this cold, flat expression and said, "So you're just going to let me lose this place?"

"I don't have it," I said again.

"You're selfish," she said. "I can't believe I raised such a selfish child."

You didn't raise me, I wanted to scream. You weren't there. You don't get to rewrite history just because it's convenient now. But I didn't say that. I just stood there, feeling like I'd failed her. Like I was the problem, again.

A few weeks later, she didn't pay rent, and when the eviction notice came, she blamed me. "If you'd helped me like you were supposed to, this wouldn't have happened." She packed her things, found somewhere else to stay, and left me scrambling. I ended up couch-surfing for a while. She didn't care. She'd gotten what she could from me, and when I couldn't give anymore, I stopped being useful. That's when I realized: she didn't want a son. She wanted a bank account with a pulse.

The thing about financial abuse is that it's invisible. There are no bruises. No scars. Just a slow erosion of your resources, your stability, your sense of self-worth. And when it's your parent doing it, it's even harder to see. Because you're supposed to help family, right? But there's a difference between helping someone and being exploited. And Mother crossed that line so many times I lost count.

Takeaway: **If someone only loves you when you're useful, that's not love—it's a transaction.**

7

THE NIGHT THEY CALLED THE POLICE ON THE VICTIM

When the person hurting you controls the narrative, the truth doesn't matter.

I lived with Father and Stepmother for four years. Those were the worst four years of my life. I moved in because I had to. Legal trouble—nothing violent, just the kind of stupid mistakes kids make when they're angry and lost and desperate for attention. The kind of trouble that gets you sent to live with the parent who's been absent your whole life, because the system assumes that any parent is better than the alternative. They were wrong.

Stepmother hated me. From the moment I walked into that house, she made it clear I was an inconvenience. She didn't yell at first. She was subtler than that. She'd make comments—little digs about how I ate too much, how I didn't clean well enough, how I was lazy or stupid or difficult. She'd sigh when I walked into a room, like my presence was exhausting. Father didn't stop her. He didn't defend me. He just let it happen.

And when he finally did try to stand up for me once, she shut it down so fast I barely had time to feel relief.

It happened at dinner. Father looked at her and said, quietly, "Don't you think that's a little harsh?" I remember the shock I felt. He was defending me. Finally. But Stepmother's face crumpled. Her eyes filled with tears. "You think I'm that bad?" she said, her voice breaking. "You think I wouldn't feed him? You think I'd let him starve?" She knew exactly how to flip the script. Father backed down immediately. She left the table. Father followed her. And I sat there, alone, understanding that I would never have an ally in that house.

After that, things got worse. Stepmother started manipulating Father into punishing me. She'd lie. Small lies at first—saying I talked back, or didn't do my chores, or broke something I didn't break. And Father, desperate to keep the peace, would believe her. He'd yell at me. Ground me. Sometimes worse. I'd try to defend myself, but it didn't matter. He'd already chosen her.

The breaking point came on a night I don't like to remember. Stepmother told Father I'd done something—I don't even remember what. It was a lie. But Father believed her, and he was furious. He came at me. I don't mean he yelled—I mean he came at me. It started in the kitchen. He grabbed an empty bucket, swung it toward my head. I blocked it, more instinct than thought, and that made him angrier. He shoved me, hard, and I went sprawling into the counter. Pain shot through my side, but I scrambled back to my feet. Then he reached for the knife block.

Time did something strange in that moment. It slowed down and sped up at the same time. I saw his hand move toward the knives. I saw his face—rage, but also something else. Something blank. And I thought: He's going to kill me. I don't know if he would have. I don't know what he was thinking. But in that moment, I believed it. And I wasn't the only one. My half-brother was there. My stepbrother. Stepmother's nephew. Three boys, all younger than me, all watching with fear in their eyes.

Stepmother stood in the doorway. She wasn't scared. She wasn't trying to stop it. She was watching. And then she said, calm as anything, "Oh look. He's not afraid of his father anymore." Not: "Stop, you're going to hurt him." Not: "This is too much." Just: He's not afraid of his father anymore. Like my refusal to let him hurt me was the thing that needed correcting.

I don't remember how it ended. I think Father shoved me out of the house. What I do remember is Stepmother calling the police. On me. I was the one who'd been attacked. I was the one with bruises forming, with a side that would ache for days. But she called the police on me.

When they arrived, she played the victim perfectly. She cried. She said I was out of control, that I'd threatened Father, that they didn't feel safe with me in the house. I tried to explain. But I was a teenager with a record, and she was a crying woman with a concerned husband nodding along behind her. Who do you think they believed?

That's what people don't understand about abuse. It's not just the violence. It's the control. The manipulation. The way the abuser rewrites reality so that they're always the victim and you're always the villain. Stepmother was a master at it. And Father was too weak, or too complicit, to stop her.

I didn't go back to that house. I couldn't. But the damage was done. I'd learned that defending yourself could be called aggression. That being hurt didn't matter if the person hurting you was better at lying. That I was alone. That no one was coming to save me. And I'd learned to be angry. So, so angry.

Takeaway: **When the abuser calls the police on the victim, the message is clear—nobody's coming to save you.**

8

CLASS CLOWN, PRIVATE STORM

The funniest kids are often the saddest.

At school, I was the class clown. I made people laugh. I disrupted class. I threw paper airplanes and cracked jokes and got sent to the principal's office more times than I could count. Teachers thought I was a troublemaker. Other kids thought I was funny. Nobody thought I was hurting.

Being funny was a survival mechanism. If I could make people laugh, they'd pay attention to me. They'd like me, or at least tolerate me. I'd exist for a reason other than being the problem. And if I was laughing, maybe I could convince myself I wasn't drowning.

But the truth is, I was barely holding it together. At home, I was walking on eggshells, trying not to set off Stepmother, trying to stay out of Father's way, trying to be invisible and visible at the same time. I was carrying the weight of abandonment, of cruelty, of words like thief and worthless and never good enough. I was carrying rage I didn't know how to process, sadness I didn't have words for, fear that lived in my chest like a second heartbeat. But at school, I couldn't show any of that. So I turned it into jokes. Into disruption. Into anything that didn't look like pain.

I got in trouble a lot. Detention. Suspension. Calls home that just made things worse. Teachers would lecture me about wasting my potential, about being a distraction, about how I needed to take things seriously. But they didn't ask why I was acting out. They didn't ask if I was okay. They just punished me and moved on. And I let them. Because explaining would've meant admitting how broken I felt. And I wasn't ready to do that.

The worst part was the loneliness. I was surrounded by people all day. I had friends, sort of—kids who laughed at my jokes, who hung out with me at lunch. But none of them really knew me. None of them saw past the performance. And I didn't let them. I kept everyone at arm's length, because closeness meant vulnerability, and vulnerability meant getting hurt. So I was alone in a crowd. Funny, but not happy. Visible, but not seen.

There were moments when the mask slipped. When I'd zone out in class, staring at nothing, feeling the weight of everything pressing down on me. When I'd snap at someone over something small, the anger spilling out before I could stop it. But those moments were brief. I'd crack another joke, force a smile, and everyone would forget. Except me. I never forgot.

Here's what I wish someone had understood: class clowns aren't just seeking attention. They're deflecting. They're hiding. They're using humor as armor because they don't have anything else. And when you punish them without asking why, you're missing the point.

I needed help. I needed someone to see through the jokes and the bravado and ask, "What's really going on?" I needed someone to connect the dots between my behavior and my circumstances, to realize that a kid acting out this much is a kid in pain. But nobody did. So I kept clowning. Kept disrupting. Kept pretending everything was fine. And inside, I kept breaking.

Takeaway: **The kid making everyone laugh might be the one most desperate for someone to ask if they're okay.**

9

THE WORST FOUR YEARS

Some houses aren't homes—they're prisons where the guards pretend to love you.

Four years. That's how long I lived with Father and Stepmother. One thousand, four hundred and sixty-one days of waking up in a place where I wasn't wanted, where every breath felt like an imposition. People say time heals. They're wrong. Sometimes time just gives you more opportunities to be wounded.

From the outside, it probably looked normal. A father trying to do right by his son. A blended family working through challenges. A teenager going through a rough patch. But inside that house, I was being slowly erased.

Stepmother was meticulous in her cruelty. She never hit me—she didn't have to. She had other tools. Words that landed like slaps. Silence that felt like suffocation. Looks that said you're nothing more clearly than any insult could. She'd criticize everything. The way I walked. The way I talked. How I ate, how I dressed, how I existed. Nothing I did was right. And when I tried to do better, she'd just find something new to pick apart. It was death by a thousand cuts. Each one small enough that you couldn't point to it and say, "This is abuse." But together, they bled me dry.

Father watched it happen. Sometimes he participated. Sometimes he just stood there, silent, letting her tear me down. He chose his peace over my protection. He chose keeping Stepmother happy over keeping me safe. He chose the easy road—silence—over the hard one: standing up for his son. And every time he made that choice, he taught me that I wasn't worth fighting for.

I developed strategies. I learned to read Stepmother's moods, to sense when a storm was coming. I learned to stay in my room as much as possible, to avoid common areas, to move through the house like a ghost. I learned to lie. To say "yes ma'am" and "no ma'am" and "I'm sorry" even when I'd done nothing wrong. To apologize for existing, because that was easier than fighting. I learned to dissociate. To let my mind drift somewhere else while my body sat through dinner, through lectures, through the endless litany of ways I was failing.

There were small mercies. My half-brother, my stepbrother, Stepmother's nephew—they weren't cruel. They were just kids, caught in the same house, trying not to become targets themselves. But they were afraid. They'd shrink back, stay quiet, make themselves small. I don't blame them. They were surviving, just like me. But it meant I was alone. Even surrounded by people, I was completely alone.

The worst part wasn't the acute moments. The worst part was the accumulation. The relentless, day-after-day grind of being told you're worthless. Because eventually, you start to believe it. You start to think: Maybe they're right. Maybe I am the problem. Maybe I am broken, defective, unlovable. You internalize their cruelty until it becomes your own inner voice. Until you don't need them to tear you down anymore—you do it yourself.

I remember one night, lying in bed, staring at the ceiling, feeling this vast emptiness inside me. Not sadness, exactly. Just nothing. Like I'd been hollowed out. I thought: This is what it feels like to give up. Not on life—I wasn't suicidal then. But on hope. On the idea that things could get better. On the belief that I deserved better. I gave up on those things. And once you give up on hope, all that's left is anger.

The anger grew slowly, like a seed planted in fertile soil. It started small—irritation, frustration, resentment. But it grew. Fed by every insult, every injustice, every moment of abandonment and cruelty. By the time I left that house, the anger was a living thing inside me. It had weight. It had teeth. And it wanted out.

Here's what people don't tell you about enduring this kind of slow erosion: it doesn't feel like surviving. It feels like disappearing. Like you're being ground down into something smaller and smaller until you're not sure anything is left. That's not strength. That's what happens when no one sees you being hurt.

When I finally left that house, I thought I was free. But I wasn't. I'd just traded one prison for another. The prison I carried inside me. Because the house was never the real problem. The problem was what it did to me. The beliefs it installed, the wounds it left, the rage it cultivated. I got out of the house. But the house never left me.

Takeaway: **Surviving abuse doesn't mean you escaped unscathed—it means you're still carrying what they did to you.**

10

THE KNIFE MOMENT

There are moments that define you—and moments you spend the rest of your life trying to forget.

I've already told you about the night Father reached for the knife block. But I haven't told you what it did to me afterward.

In the days and weeks after, I kept replaying it. Over and over. His hand reaching. The boys watching. Stepmother standing there, saying those words: He's not afraid of his father anymore. And I'd think: What if he'd grabbed it? What if he'd actually picked up the knife? Would he have used it? Would I be alive right now? I don't know. I'll never know. But the not-knowing is its own kind of torture.

What I do know is this: I believe Stepmother would've spun it. If Father had killed me that night, she would've made it about self-defense. She would've said I attacked him first. She would've cried to the police, painted me as violent, dangerous, out of control. And those boys—my half-brother, my stepbrother, her nephew—they would've backed her up. Not because they wanted to, but because they were kids, and she had power, and lying would've been easier than telling the truth. I would've been dead and blamed for my own death.

That realization changed something in me. Up until that point, I still believed, on some level, that adults had limits. That someone, somewhere, would step in if things got too bad. But that night shattered that belief. I learned that adults could hurt you as much as they wanted. That they could justify anything. And I learned that I was the only one who was going to protect me.

The anger after that was different. It wasn't just resentment or frustration anymore. It was something colder. Something sharper. I started thinking about what I'd do if it happened again. I thought about exits. About what I was capable of. About things I'm not proud of.

I need to be clear: I never hurt anyone. I never acted on those thoughts. But having them scared me. Because I wasn't just angry. I was fantasizing about violence. About revenge. And that's when I realized: I was becoming dangerous. Not to them—not yet. But to myself. Because carrying that much rage, that much hurt, without any outlet or help or way to process it—it doesn't just sit there. It festers. It grows. It starts looking for a way out.

People talk about trauma like it's something that happens to you. And it is. But it's also something that changes you. Something that rewires your brain, your instincts, your understanding of the world. That night rewired me. It taught me that safety is an illusion. That trust is a weakness. That the only person you can count on is yourself.

I think about the boys who were there. I wonder what they remember. I wonder if they're okay. If they got out. I hope they got help. I hope someone told them that what they witnessed wasn't normal, wasn't okay, wasn't their fault. Because nobody told me that. And I spent years thinking I was the problem.

The knife moment was a turning point. Not because it was the worst thing that happened—though it was close. But because it was the moment I realized I had a choice: I could let this destroy me, or I could find a way to survive it without becoming a monster. I didn't make that choice right away. It took years. But the seed was planted that night. And eventually, it grew into something that saved my life.

Takeaway: **Surviving violence doesn't mean you're safe—it**

means you're carrying a wound that needs healing before it infects everything.

11

THE THOUGHT I'M NOT PROUD OF

The most dangerous thoughts are the ones we keep secret. I need to tell you something I've never said out loud. Something I'm ashamed of, but that I think is important for you to know. There was a time, years after I left that house, when I thought about killing them. Not in a vague, passive way. In a specific, detailed, calculated way. I thought about going back to that house in the middle of the night. I thought about them asleep, unaware. I thought about ending it—the pain, the rage, the memories that wouldn't leave me alone. I thought about it more than once.

I'm not telling you this to shock you. I'm telling you because it's the truth. And because I know I'm not the only person who's ever had thoughts like this. When you're carrying that much unhealed trauma, that much rage, that much pain—it has to go somewhere. And if you don't have healthy ways to process it, it goes to dark places. It whispers to you. It tells you that the only way to make the pain stop is to make them stop. It tells you that you'd be justified, that they deserve it, that nobody would blame you if they knew what you'd been through. It tells you lies. And if you're not careful, you start believing them.

I never acted on those thoughts. I need to be absolutely clear about that. I never hurt anyone. I never made a plan beyond the fantasy. But having the thoughts at all terrified me. Because I realized: I was closer to becoming a monster than I wanted to admit. The line between thought and action isn't as solid as we like to believe. And if I didn't get help, I might cross it. And once you cross it, you can't come back.

That's what untreated trauma does. It doesn't just hurt you. It turns you into someone who might hurt others. Not because you're a bad person, but because pain that big, that unprocessed, that ignored —it becomes toxic. It becomes poison. And poison spreads. I was poisoned. And I was starting to realize that if I didn't find an antidote, I was going to infect everything I touched.

I think about the people who don't realize this in time. The ones who let the rage build and build until it explodes. The ones who end up in the news, and everyone asks, "How could they do that?" as if it's incomprehensible. It's not incomprehensible. It's predictable. When you take a child and hurt them, reject them, abandon them, abuse them—and then you offer them no help, no support, no tools to process that pain—you're creating a bomb. And you're just hoping it doesn't go off.

I'm not excusing violence. I'm not saying that trauma justifies hurting others. It doesn't. Ever. But I am saying that we need to stop pretending like these things come out of nowhere. They don't. They come from years of compounding pain, of cries for help that went unanswered, of a system that punishes people for being hurt instead of helping them heal.

What saved me wasn't willpower. It wasn't strength. It wasn't some innate goodness that kept me from crossing the line. What saved me was fear. I was afraid of who I was becoming. I was afraid of the thoughts in my head. I was afraid that if I didn't do something, I'd end up doing something I couldn't undo. And that fear, as painful as it was, was a gift. Because it made me realize: I needed help.

Here's what I want you to understand: if you've ever had thoughts like mine, it doesn't mean you're a monster. It means you're in pain. It means you're carrying something too heavy to carry alone. And it means you need help. Desperately. Urgently. Before the thoughts become actions.

The thought I'm not proud of was a symptom. A symptom of untreated trauma, of pain that had nowhere to go, of rage that was eating me alive. And the moment I recognized it as a symptom, instead of as proof that I was irredeemable, was the moment I started to heal. I got help. And it saved my life. And probably someone else's life, too.

Takeaway: **The thoughts you're most ashamed of are the ones you need to talk about before they become something worse.**

THE DECISION

The space between hitting bottom and choosing differently.

I want to tell you about the day I finally made the call.

It wasn't dramatic. There was no rock-bottom moment caught on film, no intervention, no person grabbing my arm before I walked off a ledge. It was a Tuesday. I was sitting in a parking lot outside a grocery store, engine running, and I hadn't gone inside yet because I couldn't make myself move. I'd been sitting there for forty-five minutes. I didn't know why. I just couldn't move.

I'd been like that for weeks—unable to start things, unable to finish them, going through the motions of a life that felt like it was happening to someone else. I was working a job I didn't care about. I was living in a place that didn't feel like home. I had people around me who thought I was fine because I was still showing up, still performing the version of myself that knew how to make people comfortable. But inside, I was carrying the thoughts from the last chapter. The specific, detailed ones. The ones that scared me. And they were getting louder.

I sat in that parking lot and I had a thought so clear it felt like a voice: If I don't do something, this is going to go somewhere I can't come back from.

Not "I should probably see someone." Not "It might help to talk to somebody." A clear, cold, factual understanding: I am in danger. Not from outside. From inside. The rage I'd been feeding for years, the thoughts I'd been keeping secret, the pain I'd been managing through performance and distance and isolation—it was reaching a pressure point. And I knew it. The way you know a tire is about to blow before it goes: you can feel it in how the car handles. Something is wrong. Something is about to give.

I pulled out my phone. I sat there for another ten minutes, staring at it. I typed "therapist near me" and then deleted it. I typed it again. I thought about every message I'd absorbed growing up: We don't do that. That's not for us. Strong people handle their own problems. Real men don't talk about their feelings. I thought about what it would mean to admit out loud, to a stranger, that I was having thoughts about violence. That I had been for a while. That I didn't trust myself. I thought: They'll lock me up. They'll call the police. They'll confirm everything everyone ever said about me—that I was dangerous, unstable, a problem.

Then I thought about the alternative. I thought about what happened to people who kept going the way I was going. I'd seen it. Men who became what they hated. Men who hurt people and couldn't explain why, or who hurt themselves because they didn't know where else to put it. Men who disappeared into anger and never came back.

I didn't want to disappear.

I hit search.

The first call I made went to voicemail. I hung up without leaving a message. The second call, someone answered. A woman with a calm voice asked how she could help me. I almost said "wrong number." Instead, I heard myself say: "I think I need to talk to someone. I've been having some thoughts I'm not proud of and I don't know what to do with them."

She didn't panic. She didn't put me on hold and call the police. She said, "That takes real courage to say out loud. Can you tell me a little more?"

That was it. That was the moment. Not the first therapy session—that came three weeks later. Not the first breakthrough—that took months. But that sentence: Can you tell me a little more? It was the first time in my life I could remember an adult responding to my pain with curiosity instead of punishment, dismissal, or silence. It cracked something open. Not dramatically. Just enough.

I went inside the grocery store after I hung up. I bought what I needed. I drove home. From the outside, it looked like nothing had happened. But I knew. Something had shifted. Not fixed—shifted. I'd told one true thing to one person who wasn't going to use it against me. And I was still alive. I was still okay.

That's the thing nobody tells you about asking for help: the first step isn't about being ready. You're never ready. The first step is just doing it anyway—terrified, ashamed, unsure—because you've run out of other options and you're tired of being dangerous to yourself.

I was twenty-three years old. It had taken me that long to make one phone call. And that phone call changed everything.

Takeaway: **You don't have to be ready to ask for help. You just have to be more afraid of what happens if you don't.**

PART III

THE REBUILD

12

THE GOD COMPLEX

The most dangerous parents are the ones who think they can't be questioned.

I was maybe fourteen the first time I tried to explain to Father that something was wrong.

Not about the violence—I knew better than to go there. Just something smaller. I'd been accused of breaking something in the house. I hadn't. I could account for exactly where I was, what I was doing, why the timeline didn't work. I laid it out as calmly as a fourteen-year-old can. I presented my case. I looked at him and said, "I didn't do it. And here's why I know I didn't."

He looked at me for a long moment. Then he said: "You don't talk to me like that."

That was the entire response. Not "let me look into it." Not "walk me through that again." Not even a refusal that engaged with what I'd said. Just: you don't talk to me like that. As if the act of explaining myself was the offense. As if having a defense was disrespectful.

That was the moment I understood how it worked. In that house, questioning an adult wasn't disagreement. It was blasphemy. And blasphemy had to be shut down before it spread.

I see that pattern everywhere now. Parents who confuse respect with fear. Who think that being questioned undermines their authority. Who believe that admitting a mistake, apologizing to their child, or allowing their child to have a perspective is weakness. Father operated from that place. His word was law. His feelings mattered; mine didn't. His authority was absolute, and any challenge to it—any question, any defense, any attempt to assert my own humanity—was rebellion to be crushed.

Stepmother took it further. She didn't just demand obedience—she demanded a particular kind of silence. Not the silence of a child who feels safe. The silence of a child who has learned that speaking costs too much. She needed to be seen as perfect, as selfless, as the victim of an ungrateful stepchild. Any suggestion that she was cruel —that was heresy. So she punished me. Not with her hands. She used Father. She used guilt. She used the system. She turned my defense into proof of my guilt, my pain into proof of my defiance.

Here's the thing about the god complex: it's fragile. Because deep down, the people who cling to it hardest are the ones most afraid of being questioned. They're afraid that if you look too closely, you'll see they're not gods at all. They're just people. Flawed, wounded, imperfect people who are doing a terrible job and can't admit it. So they double down. They demand louder. They punish harder. They make it so terrifying to question them that you stop trying. And in doing so, they prove that they were never worthy of godhood in the first place.

I used to think that breaking the cycle meant being a perfect parent. That I had to get everything right, never make mistakes, never hurt my future kids the way I was hurt. But that's just another version of the god complex. Breaking the cycle doesn't mean being perfect. It means being human. It means admitting when you're wrong. It means listening when your child says they're hurt. It means choosing connection over control. It means remembering that you're raising a person, not a subject.

That fourteen-year-old standing in front of Father, laying out his case, was doing something right. He was trying to be heard. He was trying to tell the truth. He was reaching for the kind of relationship where words matter and evidence counts and people are treated with basic fairness. He didn't get it. But I still think he was right to try.

Takeaway: **Parents who act like gods raise children who grow up feeling like they were never allowed to be human.**

13

THERAPY ISN'T FOR "CRAZY"— IT'S FOR THE WOUNDED

Asking for help isn't weakness—it's the bravest thing you can do.

I was in my twenties when I finally went to therapy. And I almost didn't go. Because everything I'd been taught told me that therapy was for other people. White people. Weak people. "Crazy" people. Not for someone like me. In the Black community I grew up in, you didn't talk to strangers about your problems. You prayed. You toughed it out. You handled it. And if you couldn't handle it, you kept that to yourself, because admitting you were struggling was admitting you were broken.

So I kept it to myself. For years. Even as the rage grew, even as the thoughts got darker, even as I felt myself slipping toward a version of myself I didn't want to become.

What changed was fear. The fear I described in the previous chapter. The parking lot. The phone call. The voice on the other end that didn't panic.

Three weeks after that call, I sat in a waiting room that smelled like vanilla and looked like someone's living room. Beige walls. A water feature in the corner that I found more annoying than calming. I filled out forms asking me to rate my anxiety on a scale of one to ten, and I thought, How do I rate this? It's been at a seven since I was nine years old.

My therapist was a Black woman in her forties. She wore reading glasses on a beaded chain and had a way of looking at you that felt like she was already two steps ahead of whatever you were about to say. I sat down across from her and she asked: "What brings you here?"

I opened my mouth and what came out was: "I've been having some thoughts that scare me."

She nodded. Didn't flinch. Didn't reach for a phone. She just said, "Tell me about them."

So I did. Not everything—not that first session. But I told her enough. I told her I'd been having thoughts about people who hurt me. That the thoughts were specific. That they'd been there for a while and were getting more detailed, not less. I watched her face while I talked, waiting for the moment her expression would shift into alarm or judgment. It didn't.

When I finished, she was quiet for a moment. Then she said:

"You're not here because you're broken. You're here because you were hurt. There's a difference."

I sat with that sentence for a long time. I'm still sitting with it.

Because I'd spent my entire life believing I was the problem. That there was something fundamentally wrong with me, something defective and unfixable. That the pain I carried was proof of my inadequacy. But she reframed it. She said: You were hurt. And hurt people need help to heal. Not fixing. Healing. Because I wasn't broken. I was wounded. And wounds don't heal on their own—they fester.

Therapy wasn't magic. It didn't fix everything overnight. It was slow, hard work. Weeks of unpacking memories I'd buried. Months of learning to name what I felt instead of just drowning in it. Years of rewriting the narratives I'd believed about myself. But it worked. Slowly, incrementally, it worked.

I learned that the anger wasn't the enemy. The anger was a messenger, telling me I'd been hurt and that I deserved better. The problem wasn't the anger—it was that I didn't know what to do with it. I learned that the thoughts I was ashamed of weren't proof that I was a monster. They were symptoms of untreated trauma. And symptoms can be treated. I learned that asking for help wasn't weakness. It was self-awareness. It was courage. It was the first step toward becoming someone I could actually live with.

Here's what I wish someone had told me earlier: Therapy isn't about being "crazy." It's about being human. Humans get hurt. Humans carry pain. Humans need help processing things that are too big to carry alone. And there's no shame in that. The shame is in suffering in silence. The shame is in letting the pain control you. The shame is in passing that pain to the next generation because you were too stubborn to deal with it.

I know the stigma is real. I know that in a lot of Black communities, therapy is still seen as something for other people. Something that means you're weak, or you've failed, or you don't have enough faith. But that stigma is killing us. It's killing our kids. It's perpetuating cycles of trauma that don't have to continue. Because here's the truth: faith is important. Prayer is important. Community is important. But none of those things replace professional help when you're dealing with trauma. You wouldn't pray away a broken leg. You'd go to a doctor. Mental and emotional wounds are the same.

Therapy saved my life. I don't say that lightly. I genuinely believe that if I hadn't gone, if I'd kept trying to handle it on my own, I'd be dead or in prison or living a half-life haunted by rage. But I went. And it was hard. And it was worth it. Because now, I'm not just surviving. I'm living. I'm healing. I'm building a life that isn't defined by what was done to me. And you can, too.

Takeaway: **Therapy isn't for the "crazy"—it's for anyone carrying pain too heavy to carry alone.**

14

BOUNDARIES, NOT BITTERNESS

You can protect yourself without becoming what hurt you.

For a long time, I thought healing meant cutting everyone off. Burning bridges. Building walls so high that nobody could ever hurt me again. I thought the only way to protect myself was to become untouchable. Hard. Cold. Bitter. And I tried. I really did. I cut off Mother. I cut off Father. I stopped talking to extended family who'd stood by and watched. I convinced myself that isolation was strength, that not needing anyone was freedom.

But isolation isn't freedom. It's just another kind of prison. And bitterness isn't protection—it's poison you drink hoping someone else dies.

In therapy, I learned the difference between boundaries and bitterness. Bitterness says: "You hurt me, so I'm going to carry this anger forever and let it define me." Boundaries say: "You hurt me, so I'm going to protect myself by limiting your access to me." Bitterness is reactive. Boundaries are proactive. They're about protecting your peace, your mental health, your future. They're about saying, "I deserve better than this, and I'm going to act accordingly."

Setting boundaries with my parents was one of the hardest things I've ever done. It required me to admit, out loud, that the relationship was harmful. That I wasn't obligated to keep people in my life just because they were family.

The conversation with Mother happened on a Sunday afternoon. She'd called asking if I could come over, said she needed to talk. I drove over knowing it would probably end with her asking for something. It did. She needed money for her phone bill, and she framed it the way she always did—soft at first, then harder when I didn't immediately agree. I sat across from her at her kitchen table, and for the first time, I didn't feel the old pull. The fear of losing her approval. The guilt. I just felt clear.

"I'm not going to be able to keep doing this," I said.

She looked up. "Keep doing what?"

"This. The calls when you need something. The warmth when I say yes and the cold when I say no. That's not a relationship. That's a transaction. And I'm stepping back from it."

She went very still. I'd expected crying. Maybe anger. Instead she said: "So you're just going to abandon me."

I noticed the word. Abandon. The word she should have used about herself twenty years earlier. "I'm not abandoning you," I said. "I'm protecting myself. There's a difference."

She didn't take it well. She tried guilt—said I was selfish, that I didn't understand how hard her life was, that a good son wouldn't do this. I held the line. Not with anger. With quiet. I told her I loved her. I told her I hoped she'd get the support she needed. And then I left.

I sat in my car for a long time after that. It felt like grief. Like officially closing a door I'd been hoping someone would open from the other side. But underneath the grief was something else—something that took me a few days to name. It was peace. Real, unfamiliar, slightly terrifying peace.

With Father, the conversation was different in tone but the same in clarity. I told him: "You chose your peace over my safety. You let her hurt me. And I can't have you in my life knowing you'd do it again." He tried anger—said I was dramatic, that I'd always been difficult, that he'd done the best he could. I told him I believed that. And I told him his best hadn't been enough. Then I ended the call.

That's how boundaries actually sound. Not dramatic. Not cruel. Just clear.

Here's what I want you to understand: boundaries aren't mean. They're not selfish. Boundaries are self-care. They're how you protect yourself from people who've proven they can't be trusted with your heart. And you're allowed to set them. Even with family. Especially with family. Because being related to someone doesn't give them the right to hurt you.

But here's the key: boundaries work best when they're not rooted in bitterness. When I first cut off my parents, I did it with anger. I wanted them to hurt. I wanted revenge disguised as self-care. And that didn't heal me. It just kept me tied to them, emotionally. But when I set boundaries from a place of peace—when I did it not to hurt them, but to protect me—everything shifted. I stopped letting them live rent-free in my head. I just let go.

Letting go doesn't mean forgetting. It means: I'm not going to let what they did define the rest of my life. It means: they don't get to have power over me anymore.

Takeaway: **Boundaries aren't walls—they're gates that let in the love you deserve and keep out the harm you don't.**

15

REPARENTING MYSELF

You can't change who raised you, but you can change who you become.

There's a phrase therapists use: "reparenting yourself." When I first heard it, I thought it sounded ridiculous. How do you parent yourself? You're already grown. The damage is done. But the more I sat with it, the more it made sense. Because the truth is, I wasn't raised right. I wasn't taught how to regulate my emotions, how to set boundaries, how to believe I was worthy of love. I wasn't given the tools I needed to be a healthy adult. So I had to learn those things myself. I had to become the parent I never had.

Reparenting isn't about blame. It's about taking responsibility for your healing. It's saying: "My parents didn't give me what I needed. That's not my fault. But it is my responsibility to give it to myself now."

I remember a specific moment in a therapy session, maybe eight months in. My therapist asked me what I would've said to my nine-year-old self after Grandmother called me a thief. It felt like a stupid exercise at first. I almost said, "I don't know, something reassuring."

But then I actually thought about it. I thought about that kid at the kitchen table, looking up at a woman he lived with, a woman who was supposed to be safety, and hearing her say: You're a thief. That's all you'll ever be.

What would I say to him?

I said it out loud in that office, quietly, like I was embarrassed: "You're not a thief. You made a mistake. Mistakes don't decide who you are. You're nine years old. You're allowed to not have it all figured out yet."

My therapist looked at me and said, "Can you say that like you mean it?"

I said it again. Louder. And something shifted. Because that's what reparenting is. It's finding the kid who got condemned and telling him the truth: you were wrong about yourself. You were told the wrong things. You can put them down now.

This was hard for me. Because the voice in my head wasn't kind. It was the echo of everyone who'd ever torn me down. You're not good enough. You're going to fail. You're a thief, a problem, a disappointment. That voice had been there so long, I thought it was mine. But it wasn't. It was theirs. And I didn't have to keep listening to it.

So I started challenging it. When it said, "You're going to fail," I'd ask: "Is that true? Or is that what they told me?" When it said, "You're not good enough," I'd ask: "By whose standard? And do I even agree with that standard?" Slowly, painfully, I started replacing their voice with my own. A voice that was honest but not cruel. A voice that held me accountable but didn't destroy me.

Reparenting also meant learning basics that most people take for granted. Like how to handle conflict without exploding. How to express needs without feeling like a burden. How to receive love without waiting for the catch. These weren't things I was taught. I had to learn them as an adult, through therapy, through books, through trial and error and a lot of painful mistakes. But I learned. And every time I did something differently—every time I chose a healthy response instead of a destructive one—it felt like proof that I wasn't doomed to repeat the cycle.

One of the biggest shifts came when I realized I could give myself the things I'd always wanted from them. I wanted someone to be proud of me. So I learned to be proud of myself. Not in an arrogant way, but in a genuine, "I'm doing my best and that's enough" way. I wanted someone to check on me, to ask how I was doing. So I started checking on myself. Literally asking myself, "How am I feeling today? What do I need?" I wanted someone to protect me. So I learned to protect myself—with boundaries, with distance from toxic people, with choices that prioritized my well-being. I became the person I'd been waiting for. And it was both heartbreaking and liberating.

Reparenting doesn't erase the past. I still carry scars. I still have moments when the old wounds ache. But I'm not the person I was. I'm not ruled by rage anymore. I'm not defined by what was done to me. I'm building something new, something mine, something that doesn't depend on them changing or apologizing or finally seeing me. I'm free. Not because they let me go, but because I let them go.

Takeaway: **You can't rewrite your childhood, but you can rewrite your future—one healthy choice at a time.**

16

WHAT I WISH SOMEONE WOULD'VE TOLD ME

The truths I needed to hear twenty years ago.

If I could go back and talk to my younger self—the kid sitting by the door, the teenager swallowing rage, the young adult fantasizing about violence—here's what I'd say.

You're not the problem. I know they told you that you were. I know you've internalized it so deeply that you can't imagine a world where it's not true. But it's not. You were a kid who needed love, stability, guidance. You didn't get it. And when you reacted to that deprivation—when you acted out, when you struggled, when you withdrew—they blamed you for it. But you weren't the problem. You were the symptom of a much bigger problem: adults who didn't know how to love you the way you needed to be loved.

It's okay to ask for help. You've been taught that asking for help is weak. That real strength means handling everything on your own. That's a lie. Real strength is admitting when you're struggling and reaching out for support. Real courage is saying, "I can't do this alone, and that's okay." You don't have to carry this by yourself. There are people who can help—therapists, counselors, mentors, friends. Let them. You're not a burden. You're a person who deserves care.

The rage you're feeling is normal. You've been hurt, abandoned, abused, dismissed. Of course you're angry. That anger is your body's way of saying, "This isn't okay. You deserve better." The anger isn't the problem. The problem is that you don't know what to do with it. And if you don't learn, it will consume you. It will turn you into someone you don't want to be. So feel the anger. Acknowledge it. But don't let it drive. Find healthy ways to release it—therapy, exercise, art, whatever works. Don't let it fester into something dangerous.

They're not going to change. You keep hoping that one day they'll wake up and realize what they did to you. That they'll apologize, make it right, become the parents you needed. They won't. Not because you don't deserve it, but because they're not capable of it. They're too wrapped up in their own pain, their own denial, their own survival mechanisms. And that's heartbreaking. But you can't wait for them to change before you start healing. You have to do it without their permission, without their acknowledgment, without their help. You have to choose yourself, even when they won't.

You're allowed to set boundaries. Even with family. Even with the people who raised you. Even if it makes them angry or hurt or confused. You're allowed to say, "This relationship is hurting me, and I need space." You're allowed to protect your peace. Setting boundaries doesn't make you a bad person. It makes you a person who values themselves enough to demand better.

Therapy isn't for "crazy people." It's for hurt people. Traumatized people. People who are carrying more than they can handle alone. Going to therapy doesn't mean you're weak or broken or beyond repair. It means you're smart enough to recognize that you need help, and brave enough to get it. Don't wait until you're in crisis. Get help now. Early intervention prevents so much suffering down the road.

You can break the cycle. You're terrified that you're going to become like them. That you'll hurt people the way you were hurt. That the cycle is inevitable. It's not. You have a choice. You can recognize the patterns, do the work to heal, and choose differently. You can be the parent you never had. The partner you deserved. The friend you needed. It won't be easy. But you can do it. And doing it will set you free.

Your pain is real, and it matters. Don't let anyone minimize it. Don't let anyone tell you to get over it, to be grateful for what you had, to stop living in the past. What happened to you was real. It left wounds. Those wounds need to be acknowledged, processed, healed. You're not being dramatic. You're not being oversensitive. You're being human.

You deserve love. Not conditional love. Not transactional love. Not love that requires you to be perfect, compliant, useful. You deserve love that sees you as you are and chooses you anyway. Love that's patient with your healing. Love that doesn't punish you for having needs. You deserve it. And one day, you'll find it. But first, you have to learn to give it to yourself.

You're going to survive this. I know it doesn't feel like it right now. I know the pain feels endless, the anger feels consuming, the hopelessness feels suffocating. But you're going to make it through. You're going to do the hard work of healing. You're going to build a life that isn't defined by what they did to you. You're going to survive. And more than that, you're going to thrive. Not because the past didn't happen. But because you refused to let it be the only thing that defines you.

TO THE PARENTS READING THIS: IF YOU SEE EVEN A GLIMPSE OF YOURSELF IN THESE PAGES, I NEED YOU TO HEAR THIS: IT'S NOT TOO LATE. IT'S NOT TOO LATE TO APOLOGIZE. TO ACKNOWLEDGE THE HARM YOU CAUSED. TO GET HELP SO YOU CAN STOP REPEATING THE CYCLE. IT'S NOT TOO LATE TO LEARN A DIFFERENT WAY. TO SEE YOUR CHILD AS A PERSON, NOT A PROBLEM. TO CHOOSE CONNECTION OVER CONTROL. YOUR CHILD DOESN'T NEED YOU TO BE PERFECT. THEY NEED YOU TO BE PRESENT. TO BE HONEST. TO BE WILLING TO DO BETTER. AND IF YOU'RE NOT WILLING TO DO THAT WORK, AT LEAST GET OUT OF THEIR WAY SO THEY CAN HEAL.

TO THE YOUNG PEOPLE READING THIS: YOU ARE NOT ALONE. YOU ARE NOT BEYOND HELP. YOU ARE NOT DOOMED TO REPEAT WHAT WAS DONE TO YOU. YOU ARE WORTHY OF LOVE, OF SAFETY, OF A LIFE THAT DOESN'T HURT. ASK FOR HELP. DO THE WORK. BREAK THE CYCLE. YOUR FUTURE SELF WILL THANK YOU.

Takeaway: **The life you're living now doesn't have to be the life you live forever—healing is possible, and you deserve it.**

APPENDIX: GETTING HELP EARLY

WHY THIS MATTERS

Throughout this book, I've shared the consequences of not getting help: the rage that builds, the thoughts that darken, and the ways untreated trauma can turn a hurt person into a harmful person. I've also shared what happened when I finally asked for help: I started healing. I started building a life worth living. I started breaking the cycle.

This appendix exists because I don't want you to wait as long as I did. I want you to get help early—before the pain becomes unbearable, before the thoughts become dangerous, before you lose more years to suffering that doesn't have to continue.

WHAT THERAPY ACTUALLY IS

Therapy is a professional relationship where a trained mental health provider helps you process emotions, navigate challenges, heal from trauma, and build healthier ways of thinking and behaving.

It's not a sign you're "crazy." It's not only for people in crisis. It's not a magic fix that solves everything instantly. It is a safe space to talk about things you can't say anywhere else. It is professional support from someone trained to help. It is an investment in your mental and emotional health.

WHAT TO EXPECT IN YOUR FIRST SESSION

Your first session typically includes paperwork about your background and goals, time getting to know your therapist, an explanation of confidentiality, and a chance to ask questions. First sessions can feel awkward. That's normal. You don't have to share everything right away—trust builds over time.

HOW TO FIND A THERAPIST

Ask for referrals from your doctor, a school counselor, friends, or trusted community members. Use online directories like Psychology Today, Therapy for Black Girls, or your insurance company's provider directory. Decide what matters to you: cultural competence, specialty, logistics, and telehealth options. It's okay if the first therapist isn't the right fit—keep looking until you find someone you feel safe with.

CULTURALLY COMPETENT CARE

For Black folks and other people of color, it's okay to want a therapist who understands your cultural context. You don't have to educate your therapist about your lived experience. Questions to ask potential therapists: "What experience do you have working with Black/POC clients?" "How do you address cultural factors in therapy?" "Are you familiar with generational trauma and its impact?"

COST AND ACCESS

If you have insurance, check your plan's mental health coverage. If you don't have insurance or it isn't affordable, look into community mental health centers, university training clinics, Open Path Collective, Employee Assistance Programs, or telehealth options. Don't let cost be the reason you don't seek help.

CRISIS SUPPORT

If you're in immediate danger—or thinking about harming yourself or someone else—reach out for help right now. Call your local emergency number or go to the nearest emergency room. Many countries have national crisis hotlines and text-based support options. If you're worried about someone else, don't keep it secret—tell a trusted adult or call a crisis line for guidance.

TO PARENTS: GETTING HELP FOR YOUR CHILD

If your child is struggling—acting out, withdrawing, expressing hopelessness, getting into trouble—please get them help. Don't wait for them to "grow out of it." Don't assume it's just a phase. Early intervention prevents so much pain. It keeps kids from internalizing the belief that they're broken. It keeps hurt from turning into rage. Your child needing help isn't a failure on your part. It's an opportunity. Take it.

FINAL THOUGHTS

Asking for help is one of the hardest, bravest things you can do—especially if you were taught it's weak. But the truth is: we all need help sometimes. Getting it early can prevent years of unnecessary suffering. You deserve support. You deserve healing. You deserve a life that isn't defined by pain. So please: ask for help. Do the work. Choose yourself. Your future self will thank you.

www.ingramcontent.com/pod-product-compliance
Lightning Source LLC
LaVergne TN
LVHW022025200926
848481LV00007B/2538
9798295713248